UNLEASHING MAXIMUM PRODUCTIVITY

Secrets to Becoming a Successful and Efficient Remote Worker

Amber Willie

*This book is dedicated to God Almighty
who has brought me this far...*

CONTENTS

INTRODUCTION

In a rapidly evolving landscape, where the traditional boundaries of work are redrawn, the concept of the workplace has transcended physical confines. The rise of remote work, driven by technological advancements and shifting global dynamics, has ushered in a new era of possibilities. Welcome to a realm where your office is wherever you are, and your potential knows no geographical bounds.

Embarking on a Productivity Odyssey

As the modern workforce embraces this digital transformation, the need for an optimal virtual workspace becomes paramount. "unlashing maximum productivity" is your starting point to not only surviving but thriving in this dynamic environment. This book serves as your compass through the unknown territory of remote work, equipping you with the insights, tools, and strategies necessary to harness the full potential of your virtual workspace.

A Symphony of Efficiency and Inspiration

Within these pages, you'll discover how to orchestrate a symphony of efficiency and inspiration, transforming your digital domain into a hub of productivity. From selecting the right equipment and mastering technology to crafting a space that ignites your creativity, we'll plunge deep into the art of curating an environment that fuels your professional growth.

Unravelling the Layers

This journey isn't solely about hardware and software—it's about unravelling the layers of effective remote work. We'll unravel the intricacies of time management, communication, and collaboration in the virtual realm. We'll delve into the psyche of successful remote workers and leaders, uncovering the secrets that set them apart.

Crafting Your Path

Whether you're a remote work veteran seeking to optimize your setup or a newcomer embarking on this transformative journey, this book is your blueprint. Our goal is simple: to empower you with the knowledge, strategies and mindset required to craft your path in the ever-evolving landscape of work.

As we embark on this exploration of unleashing maximum productivity, i want you know that you hold the keys to unlocking your full potential. I am are determined to help you sculpt a productive and digital workspace that not only meets the demands of the digital age but propels you toward unparalleled success.

CHAPTER 1

Choosing the Perfect
Remote Workspace

When it comes to setting up your home office, one of the most important factors to consider is finding the ideal spot. This decision can greatly influence your productivity and efficiency.

Finding the ideal Spot:

Start by evaluating different areas in your home that could potentially serve as your workspace. Look for a location that offers privacy and minimal distractions. You must consider factors such as noise levels, foot traffic, and proximity to common areas in your home.

It's also important to choose a spot that has good natural lighting. This is because natural light improves your mood and also helps reduce eye strain and fatigue. A location near a window or adding additional lighting fixtures to ensure a well-lit workspace is important.

Creating a Productive and Comfortable Environment:

Once you've found the perfect location, it's time to set up your workspace to maximize productivity and comfort.

● Start by selecting a desk and chair that are ergonomically designed to support your body during long hours of work. This will help prevent back pain and other discomforts associated with poor posture.

● Consider the layout of your office and how it can enhance your workflow.

● Keep essential items within reach, such as your computer, phone, and stationery.

● Organize cables and cords to avoid clutter and create a clean and organized environment.

● Also, personalize your workspace to make it a place where you feel motivated and inspired.

● Add decorations, plants, or artwork that reflect your personality and create a positive atmosphere.

The Impact of Lighting on Productivity

Proper lighting plays a crucial role in creating a productive and efficient home office environment. It not only affects our vision and overall well-being but also has a significant impact on our productivity levels throughout the day. The impact of lighting on productivity is mind-blowing.

Understanding The Importance Of Proper Lighting In Your Home Office

When setting up your home office, it's essential to understand the importance of proper lighting. Insufficient or harsh lighting can lead to eye strain, headaches, and fatigue, making it difficult to focus and concentrate on your work. On the other hand, adequate lighting can enhance your mood, increase alertness, regulate your circadian rhythm, promotes vitamin D synthesis, and reduces the risk of eye strain as well as improve overall productivity.

Natural light is often considered the best source of lighting for any workspace. It not only provides a sense of connection to the outside world but also offers numerous health benefits as earlier stated. Therefore, position your desk near a window or in a location that allows natural light to flow into your workspace effortlessly.

Maximizing Natural Light and Incorporating Artificial Lighting

To maximize natural light in your home office, consider the following tips;

● Use light-coloured or reflective surfaces that can bounce light around the room.

● Avoid placing heavy curtains or blinds that block sunlight from entering your workspace. Instead, opt for light filtering or sheer curtains that allow natural light to pass through while still providing privacy.

In addition to natural light, incorporating artificial lighting is crucial for maintaining consistent illumination throughout the day, especially during darker hours or cloudy days.

● Use a combination of overhead lighting, task lighting, and ambient lighting to create a well-lit and balanced workspace.

● The use of adjustable desk lamps or LED lights

with flexible colour temperatures can provide flexibility in creating the right lighting conditions for different tasks and times of the day.

● It is essential to position your artificial lighting sources strategically to minimize glare and shadows on your work surface.

● Avoid placing lights directly above or behind your computer screen to prevent screen glare and eye strain.

● Experiment with different lighting setups to find the perfect balance that suits your needs and enhances your productivity.

CHAPTER 2

Essential Tools and Equipment

Essential Tools and Equipment are the fundamental elements required to create a successful remote work setup. By comprehending and utilizing these tools effectively, remote workers and job seekers can optimize their workspace, leading to enhanced efficiency and a streamlined workflow contributing to a more productive remote work experience.

Technology Must-Haves

As a remote worker, there are several necessary technologies that you must have to effectively carry out your work. Here is a list of essential technology must-haves:

1. A reliable and up-to-date computer is crucial for remote work. Choose a device that meets your specific needs, whether it's a laptop or desktop.

2. Monitor: Having an additional monitor or a larger screen

can significantly improve your productivity by allowing you to multitask and view multiple applications simultaneously.

3. Keyboard and Mouse: Invest in a comfortable and ergonomic keyboard and mouse to prevent strain and discomfort during long hours of typing and navigating.

4. High-Speed Internet Connection: A stable and fast internet connection is essential for remote work. Ensure that you have a reliable internet service provider and consider a backup option in case of any connectivity issues.

5. Headsets and Webcams: High-quality headsets and webcams are essential for virtual meetings and communication with colleagues and clients. Look for noise-cancelling features and clear audio quality.

6. Mobile Devices: Depending on your job requirements, having a smartphone or tablet with the necessary apps and connectivity options can be beneficial for remote work on the go.

7. Cloud Storage and File-Sharing Services: Utilize cloud storage platforms like Google Drive, Dropbox, or Microsoft OneDrive to securely store and share files with teammates and access them from any device.

8. Collaboration Tools: Use collaboration tools such as project

management software, communication platforms like Slack or Microsoft Teams, and video conferencing tools like Zoom or Microsoft Teams to collaborate effectively with your team.

9. VPN (Virtual Private Network): If your work involves handling sensitive data or accessing company resources, a VPN can provide a secure connection and protect your online privacy.

10. Cybersecurity Software: Protect your devices and data with reliable antivirus software, firewalls, and other cybersecurity measures to safeguard against potential threats.

It is advisable to regularly update your software and devices to ensure optimal performance and security while working remotely.

Organizational Tools

As a remote worker, several organizational tools can help you stay productive, effectively manage your tasks, communicate with your team, and stay organized. These organizational tools are;

1. Project Management Software: Tools like Trello, Asana, or Monday.com allow you to create and manage tasks, set deadlines, collaborate with team members, and track progress.

2. Communication Tools: Apps like Slack or Microsoft Teams enable real-time communication with your team, allowing you to

chat, make video or voice calls, and share files.

3. Time Management Apps: Tools such as RescueTime or Toggl help you track your time and analyze how you spend it, allowing you to identify areas for improvement and increase productivity.

4. Cloud Storage: Services like Google Drive, Dropbox, or OneDrive provide secure and accessible storage for your files, allowing you to access and share documents from anywhere.

5. Video Conferencing Tools: Platforms like Zoom, Google Meet, or Microsoft Teams facilitate virtual meetings, presentations, and webinars, enabling effective communication and collaboration with your team.

6. Note-Taking Apps: Tools like Evernote or OneNote help you capture and organize your thoughts, ideas, and important information, allowing you to access them from any device.

7. Password Managers: Applications such as LastPass or Dashlane securely store and manage your passwords, saving you time and ensuring your online accounts are protected.

8. Calendar and Scheduling Tools: Apps like Google Calendar or Microsoft Outlook allow you to organize your schedule, set reminders, and share availability with colleagues, ensuring efficient time management.

9. Virtual Whiteboards: Tools like Miro or Mural provide virtual collaboration spaces where you can brainstorm ideas, create visual presentations, and collaborate with team members in real-time.

10. Task and Project Tracking Tools: Platforms such as Jira or Basecamp help you track the progress of your tasks and projects, assign responsibilities, and monitor deadlines.

Summarily, by integrating these tools and equipment into your remote work arrangement, you can cultivate an atmosphere conducive to concentration and innovation. Thereby enabling peak performance and goal attainment.

Remember you don't need to acquire them all at once; newcomers to remote work can gradually assemble their toolkits. Whether you're embarking on your remote work journey or seeking to initiate one, remember that patience is a valuable resource. As you gather tools and build skills and experience, you'll steadily enhance your remote work capacities.

CHAPTER 3

Creating a Productive Routine

Creating a productive routine involves establishing a consistent work schedule, incorporating morning and pre-work rituals, as well as implementing effective time management strategies. Here is a clear explanation of each aspect:

- **Establishing a Consistent Work Schedule:**

Setting a consistent work schedule helps create structure and discipline in your remote work routine. You must also determine your choice of working hours and stick to them as closely as possible. This consistency allows you to establish a routine. Which in turn helps you manage expectations with colleagues or clients, and ensures you allocate dedicated time for work-related tasks.

- **The Power of Morning and Pre-Work Rituals:**

Morning and pre-work rituals are activities you engage in before starting your workday to set a positive tone and prepare yourself mentally and physically. These rituals can include activities such as exercise, meditation, journaling, or reading. By incorporating these rituals into your routine, you can enhance focus, reduce stress, and boost productivity.

- **Effective Time Management Strategies:**

Effective time management is crucial for remote workers to prioritize tasks, avoid procrastination, and maintain productivity. Some strategies include:

➢ Prioritizing Tasks: Identify the most important and urgent tasks and tackle them first. Use techniques like the Eisenhower Matrix (categorizing tasks into urgent, important, not urgent, and not important) to prioritize effectively.

➢ Time Blocking: Allocate specific blocks of time for different tasks or activities. This helps create a structured schedule and prevents distractions from derailing your focus.

➢ Pomodoro Technique: Break your work into focused intervals, typically 25 minutes of work followed by a short break. This technique helps maintain concentration and prevent burnout.

➢ Avoiding Multitasking: Focus on one task at a time to maximize productivity and reduce errors. Multitasking can lead to decreased efficiency and increased stress., especially when you are just getting started and still learning to navigate remote work.

➤   Setting Realistic Deadlines: Set realistic deadlines for tasks and projects, considering your available time and resources. This helps manage expectations and prevents overwhelm.

➤   Taking Regular Breaks: Incorporate regular breaks into your workday to rest and recharge. Short breaks can improve focus and productivity in the long run.

By establishing a consistent work schedule, incorporating morning and pre-work rituals, and implementing effective time management strategies, you can create a productive routine that optimizes your remote work experience.

How to manage an uninvited guest during your busy work time or deadlines

Managing an uninvited guest during your busy work time or deadlines requires a delicate approach to ensure your focus remains intact while maintaining politeness. Here's how to handle the situation effectively:

●   Acknowledge Politely: Greet the guest with a friendly acknowledgement, showing that you're aware of their presence.

●   Signal Your Busyness: Politely mention that you're currently engaged in work or have an impending deadline.

• **Express Appreciation:** Thank them for stopping by and convey that you value their visit.

• **Suggest a Specific Time:** Offer a specific time when you'll be available for a chat or interaction, showing your willingness to connect later.

• **Offer Alternatives:** If the matter is urgent, suggest alternative sources of help or assistance that the guest can turn to.

• **Body Language:** Maintain a focused posture, such as continuing to work or keeping your gaze on your screen, to signal your busyness.

• **Use Humor:** Lightly inject humor by saying something like, "I'm in the middle of solving this puzzle called work, can we catch up in a bit?"

• **Set Expectations:** Politely explain that you have an important task to complete and that you'll be fully available after you've met your deadline.

• **Stay Professional:** Keep your tone respectful and professional throughout the interaction.

• **Privacy Mode:** If you're working virtually, consider setting your status to "Do Not Disturb" or indicating that you're busy on your communication platform.

• Redirect: If the visitor insists on chatting, gently steer the conversation back to the purpose of their visit and your availability later.

• Boundaries: Emphasize the importance of respecting each other's work commitments and time.

you must knowthat the goal is to manage the situation without causing offense while ensuring your work remains a priority. Balancing politeness with assertiveness is key to maintaining your productivity and managing uninvited guests during critical work times or deadlines.

CHAPTER 4

Managing Distractions and Staying Focused

Identifying Common Remote Work Distractions

This section focuses on helping individuals identify common distractions that can arise while working remotely.

"Christopher Columb says by prevailing over all obstacles and distractions, one may unfailingly arrive at his chosen goal or destination".

And working remotely is not an easy ride because you are more susceptible to distractions. And this should be avoided at all cost. However, you can't deal with them if you don't identify them. Below are some common distractions:

- Social Media: The temptation to check social media platforms like Facebook, Instagram, or Twitter can be a significant distraction during remote work. Notifications and the urge to stay updated can disrupt focus and productivity.

- Personal Phone Calls: Personal phone calls, whether from friends or family members, can interrupt workflow and divert attention away from work-related tasks.

- Household Chores: Being at home may lead to the temptation to engage in household chores, such as cleaning, laundry, or cooking, which can easily distract from work responsibilities.

- Noisy Environments: Working from home can sometimes mean dealing with noise from family members, roommates, pets, or construction outside, all of which can disrupt concentration and focus.

Strategies To Minimize Interruptions

This section provides strategies to minimize interruptions and create a more focused work environment. Some effective strategies include:

- Establishing Boundaries: Communicate to family members, roommates, or anyone else sharing your living space about your work schedule and the importance of minimizing interruptions during designated work hours.

- Creating a Dedicated Workspace: Designate a specific area in your home as your workspace. This helps create a physical separation between work and personal life, making it easier to focus and avoid distractions.

- Using Noise-Canceling Headphones: Investing in noise-cancelling headphones can help block out external noise and create a more peaceful and focused work environment.

- Utilizing Productivity Apps: There are various productivity apps available that can help minimize distractions. These apps can block access to social media sites, limit notifications, and provide focus-enhancing features.

Techniques For Maintaining Concentration

This section provides techniques to maintain concentration and stay focused during remote work. Some effective techniques include:

- Pomodoro Technique: The Pomodoro Technique involves working in focused intervals, typically 25 minutes, followed by a short break of 5 minutes. This technique helps maintain focus and productivity by breaking work into manageable chunks.

- Task Prioritization: Prioritizing tasks and breaking them down into smaller, manageable steps can help maintain focus. By focusing on one task at a time, individuals can avoid feeling overwhelmed and stay on track.

- Visualization Exercises: Visualizing the successful completion of tasks or projects can enhance motivation and concentration. Taking a moment to visualize desired outcomes can help maintain focus and increase productivity.

Finally, Avoid being engulfed by work; remote work can lead individuals to neglect themselves due to the flexibility to work at any time. Break down your tasks, allocate short breaks to recharge, and make time for spiritual reflection/meditation, which can also provide rejuvenation.

CHAPTER 5

*Health and Well-Being in
the Home Office*

Importance of Ergonomics for Physical Health

Ergonomics is crucial for safeguarding your physical well-being while working remotely. Designing your workspace with ergonomic principles in mind ensures that your body maintains a healthy posture and minimizes strain.

Proper ergonomics involves adjusting your chair height, desk setup, monitor placement, keyboard and mouse positioning, and even lighting conditions to prevent discomfort and potential injuries like back pain, neck strain, or carpal tunnel syndrome. By prioritizing ergonomics, you enhance your comfort, reduce the risk of repetitive stress injuries, and promote overall physical health during your remote work hours.

Incorporating Movement and Exercise into Your Day

Sedentary behavior is a common pitfall of remote work. This can lead to a host of health issues. Incorporating movement and exercise into your daily routine is essential for counteracting the negative effects of prolonged sitting. You are encouraged to set regular intervals to stand, stretch, or walk around. Consider integrating short exercise routines or stretching sessions throughout the day to maintain blood circulation, flexibility, and muscle strength. Engaging in physical activity not only enhances your physical health but also boosts your energy levels, concentration, and overall well-being, contributing to a more productive and fulfilling remote work experience.

Mental Health Practices: Stress Relief and Mindfulness

Remote work comes with its own set of stressors. These include isolation, blurred boundaries between work and personal life, and increased screen time. prioritizing

That's why prioritizing mental health practices is vital for maintaining emotional well-being. As a remote worker, Implement stress relief techniques such as deep breathing, meditation, or progressive muscle relaxation to alleviate tension and anxiety.

Note that mindfulness exercises help you stay present, reduce stress, and improve your ability to focus. Creating designated breaks for relaxation, pursuing hobbies, or spending time outdoors can contribute to a healthier work-life balance. By nurturing your mental health, you enhance your resilience, creativity, and overall mental clarity, ensuring a positive remote work experience.

*For more on stress relief and management get it from my book at this link...*here

CHAPTER 6

Networking and Building
a Remote Career

Building a remote career goes beyond just finding a job; it involves strategically connecting with professionals, creating an influential online presence, and effectively navigating remote job interviews and onboarding. This chapter is dedicated to providing you with a comprehensive understanding of how networking plays a pivotal role in shaping a successful remote career.

- **Leveraging Online Platforms for Job Search and Networking**

Leveraging online platforms for job search and networking involves a strategic approach to utilizing digital resources to connect with professionals, discover job opportunities, and build a meaningful online presence. Here's a step-by-step guide:

➤ Optimize Your Profile: Start by creating a polished and complete profile on professional networking platforms like LinkedIn. Highlight your skills, experiences, achievements, and aspirations. Use a professional profile picture and craft a compelling headline that showcases your expertise.

➢ Research and Identity: Use keywords relevant to your desired role or industry to search for companies, professionals, and groups that align with your interests. Follow companies and join groups related to your field.

➢ Engage and Interact: Participate in group discussions, comment on posts, and share relevant articles. Engage in meaningful conversations to showcase your knowledge and establish your online presence.

➢ Connect Strategically: Send personalized connection requests to professionals you admire, colleagues from past jobs, and others within your industry. In your request, mention a common interest or explain why you'd like to connect.

➢ Networking Events: Many online platforms host virtual networking events, webinars, and workshops. Participate in these events to expand your network, learn from experts, and stay updated on industry trends.

➢ Share Content: Share articles, blog posts, or insights on industry topics. Regularly posting valuable content can help you establish your expertise and attract the attention of potential employers.

➢ Job Search Filters: Use job search filters on platforms like LinkedIn, Indeed, or specialized job boards to narrow down job listings based on your preferences, such as remote work, location, industry, and job level.

➢ Apply Strategically: Tailor your resume and cover letter to match the job description. Highlight relevant skills and experiences that align with the role. If possible, research the company and mention why you're interested in working there.

➢Utilize Recommendations: Request recommendations from colleagues, supervisors, or clients you've worked with in the past. Positive recommendations can enhance your credibility and showcase your abilities.

➢ Direct Outreach: If you find a company you're interested in, consider sending a personalized message to a relevant employee, expressing your admiration for their work and your interest in the company. This proactive approach can create opportunities for networking and informational interviews.

➢ Attend Virtual Conferences: Participate in virtual conferences, workshops, and webinars relevant to your industry. These events provide opportunities to learn, connect with professionals, and showcase your enthusiasm for your field.

Stay Consistent: Consistency is key. Regularly update your profile, engage with your network, and continue expanding your connections. Networking is an ongoing process that requires nurturing.

Building a Strong Online Presence and Personal Brand

Building a strong online presence and personal brand requires a thoughtful and strategic approach. Here are key tips to help you effectively establish and enhance your digital identity:

1. Define Your Brand Identity: Clarify your unique value proposition, strengths, and passions. Understand what sets you apart from others in your field and how you want to be perceived by your target audience.

2. Consistent Messaging: Maintain a consistent message across all your online profiles and interactions. Your bio, headlines, and content should align with your brand identity and reflect your expertise.

3. Professional Profile Photo: Use a high-quality and professional profile photo. A clear and friendly image can help make a positive first impression and humanize your online presence

4. Craft an Elevator Pitch: Develop a concise and compelling elevator pitch that succinctly describes who you are, what you

do, and the value you bring. Use this in your online bios and introductions.

5. Optimize Social Media Profiles: Customize your social media profiles to reflect your brand identity. Use keywords related to your industry, and ensure your profiles are public and easily discoverable.

6. Content Sharing: Share valuable and relevant content that showcases your expertise. This could include articles, blog posts, industry news, or your insights on trending topics.

7. Engage Authentically: Engage in meaningful conversations with your network. Respond to comments, ask questions, and offer insights to demonstrate your knowledge and passion.

8. Networking: Actively connect with professionals in your industry, colleagues, mentors, and potential employers. Send personalized connection requests with a brief note explaining your interest in connecting.

9. Publish Original Content: If possible, create and share original content, such as blog posts, videos, or infographics. This establishes you as an authority and allows you to share your unique perspective.

10. Showcase Achievements: Highlight your accomplishments,

projects, and milestones. Share success stories and case studies to demonstrate your capabilities.

11. Recommendations and Endorsements: Request recommendations and endorsements from colleagues, supervisors, and clients. Positive testimonials add credibility to your brand.

12. Video Content: Consider creating and sharing video content. Video allows you to connect on a more personal level and can be a powerful way to convey your expertise.

Participate in Online Communities: Join relevant online forums, groups, and communities where you can share your knowledge, ask questions, and connect with others in your field.

13. Continuous Learning: Stay updated with the latest industry trends, news, and developments. Sharing your insights on emerging topics can position you as a thought leader.

14. Offline Networking: While online presence is crucial, don't overlook offline networking opportunities. Attend industry events, conferences, and workshops to connect with professionals face-to-face.

Building a strong online presence and personal brand takes time and consistency. Be authentic, showcase your expertise, and engage genuinely with your network to create a lasting and impactful digital identity.

Navigating Remote Interviews

Remote interviews and onsite interviews are two distinct formats used by employers to assess candidates during the hiring process.

In recent years, remote interviews have become more common due to technological advancements and the global shift toward remote work. Both types of interviews aim to evaluate a candidate's qualifications, skills, and cultural fit, but they offer distinct experiences and challenges based on the format and location of the interview.

The difference between remote and Onsite interviews

	Remote	Onsite
1	Location: Remote interviews take place virtually, typically over video conferencing platforms like Zoom, Skype, or Microsoft Teams.	Location: Onsite interviews occur at the physical premises of the company or a designated interview location.
2	Geographical Flexibility: Candidates and interviewers can participate from different locations, eliminating the need for travel.	Travel: Candidates need to travel to the interview location, which may require additional time and expenses.
3	Setup: Candidates need a computer or mobile device with a camera, microphone, and stable internet	Setup: Candidates interact face-to-face with interviewers. The dress code is usually more formal

	connection. They should also ensure a quiet and well-lit space for the interview.	and covers the entire outfit.
4	Attire: The dress code remains professional, but there may be more flexibility since only the upper half of the body is visible in most video calls.	
5	Interaction: Communication is through digital means, which may affect non-verbal cues and body language. Candidates must ensure clear and effective communication over the Internet.	Interaction: In-person interactions allow interviewers to assess non-verbal cues, body language, and the candidate's overall presence more effectively.
6	Environment Control: Candidates have more control over their interview environment and can display relevant materials on their screen if allowed.	Environment Control: Candidates have limited control over the interview environment, as they are in a designated space.
7	Logistics: Technical issues, such as internet connectivity problems, can impact the interview experience. Both parties should be prepared for potential technical hiccups.	Logistics: Onsite interviews are less prone to technical issues, but they require careful planning for travel, directions, and punctuality.

In recent years, remote interviews have become more common due to technological advancements and the global shift toward remote work. Both types of interviews aim to evaluate a candidate's qualifications, skills, and cultural fit, but they offer distinct experiences and challenges based on the format and location of the interview.

Samples of difficult remote interview questions

Remote interviews can present unique challenges, and certain questions may require thoughtful responses to demonstrate your suitability for the role and your adaptability to remote work. Here are some potentially difficult remote interview questions along with tips on how to answer them effectively:

How do you stay motivated and productive while working remotely?

Tip: Share specific strategies you use to maintain focus, such as setting clear goals, creating a structured daily routine, and minimizing distractions. Provide examples of times you've successfully managed your time and tasks remotely.

How do you handle communication and collaboration with team members when you're not physically present?

Tip: Discuss your proficiency with virtual communication tools (e.g., Slack, video conferencing), and highlight instances where you've effectively communicated and collaborated with remote team members. Emphasize your proactive approach to maintaining open lines of communication.

Can you give an example of a project you've completed remotely?

Tip: Share a specific project where you had to coordinate with team members from different locations. Describe the challenges you faced and how you overcame them, highlighting your ability to work independently and contribute to a remote team's success.

How do you ensure work-life balance while working remotely?

Tip: Explain your strategies for setting clear boundaries between work and personal life, such as establishing a designated workspace, scheduling breaks, and unplugging after work hours. Mention your commitment to maintaining your well-being to ensure sustained productivity.

What steps do you take to stay updated and connected with industry trends while working remotely?

Tip: Discuss how you actively engage in online industry forums, attend virtual webinars, and read relevant publications to stay informed. Provide examples of how you've applied new knowledge to your work or projects.

How do you handle technical challenges or disruptions during remote work?

Tip: Share instances when you encountered technical issues while working remotely and explain how you troubleshoot and resolved them. Highlight your resourcefulness and ability to adapt to unexpected situations.

Describe a time when you faced a communication misunderstanding while working remotely. How did you handle it?

Tip: Narrate a situation where miscommunication occurred and explain how you clarified the issue through active listening, asking questions, and using written communication effectively. Highlight your problem-solving skills in resolving remote communication challenges.

What strategies do you use to build rapport and relationships with remote colleagues or clients?

Tip: Describe how you initiate informal conversations, engage in virtual team-building activities, and express genuine interest in your colleagues' well-being. Share examples of times when you successfully established strong connections despite the physical distance.

When answering these questions, focus on providing specific examples from your past experiences that highlight your skills, adaptability, and success in a remote work environment. Tailor your responses to showcase how you've effectively managed remote work challenges and contributed to positive outcomes.

Must watch out when looking for remote opportunities

When engaging in remote work opportunities, it's essential to be vigilant and aware of potential red flags that could indicate issues with the job, employer, or work environment. Here are some red flags to pay attention to:

1. Lack of Clear Communication: If the employer or team

members are unresponsive, provide vague instructions, or fail to communicate effectively, it can hinder your ability to perform your tasks and collaborate efficiently.

2. Unrealistic Expectations: Be cautious if the job description or expectations seem too good to be true. Promises of high pay with minimal effort or unrealistic goals could indicate a potential scam or unreliable employer.

3. Unclear Work Arrangements: If the terms of your employment, compensation, or responsibilities are unclear or subject to frequent changes, it may signal a lack of organization or potential issues down the line.

4. Unprofessional Interview or Hiring Process: If the interview process is disorganized, unprofessional, or lacks transparency, it may indicate a disregard for professionalism and employee well-being.

5. Pressure to Share Personal Information: Be wary if you're asked to share sensitive personal or financial information before a formal offer is made. Legitimate employers should not require this.

6. Request for Upfront Payment or Investment: *Any job that asks you to pay a fee or make an upfront investment to secure the position is likely a scam.*

7. Inadequate Technology and Tools: If the employer doesn't provide the necessary tools, software, or equipment to perform your remote tasks effectively, it could impact your productivity and job satisfaction.

8. Unusual Payment Methods: Be cautious if the employer asks you to receive payments through unconventional methods, such as personal bank accounts or cryptocurrency.

Isolation from Colleagues: If you're consistently isolated from other team members or 9. discouraged from communicating with colleagues, it could be a sign of a lack of team collaboration or a toxic work environment.

10. Unreasonable Demands: Watch out for excessive workloads, requests for after-hours availability, or unreasonable demands that could lead to burnout.

11. No Online Presence or Reviews: A lack of online presence or credible reviews of the company or employer might indicate that they're not well-established or reputable.

12. Negative Reviews or Reports: Research the company online and check for negative reviews, reports of unethical practices, or legal issues before committing to a remote job.

13. Frequent Payment Delays: Consistent delays in receiving

payments or inconsistent payment methods can indicate financial instability or potential payment issues.

14. Pressure to Sign Contracts Quickly: If you're pressured to sign contracts or agreements hastily without ample time to review or seek legal advice, it could indicate hidden terms or conditions.

Trust your instincts and conduct thorough research before committing to any remote work opportunity. If something feels off or if you encounter multiple red **flags, it's advisable to proceed with caution or seek guidance from trusted sources before moving forward.**

Onboarding Processes in a remote setting

In a Remote setting, the onboarding process is adapted to accommodate the virtual nature of work and to ensure that new employees can seamlessly integrate into the company from a distance. Here's what you can expect from the onboarding process in a remote setting:

1. Virtual Orientation:

• Instead of an in-person tour, you'll receive a virtual introduction to the company's culture, values, and mission.

• You'll learn about the tools, software, and communication platforms used for remote work.

2. Digital Paperwork and Documentation:

• Complete necessary paperwork online, including tax forms, benefits enrollment, and compliance documents.

• Obtain access to company systems, emails, and digital resources remotely.

3. Virtual Training and Skill Development:

• Participate in online training modules and webinars tailored to your role and responsibilities.

• Learn about job-specific tasks, company processes, and expectations through digital resources.

4. Remote Team Integration:

• Interact with team members through video conferencing, instant messaging, and collaboration tools.

• Schedule virtual one-on-one or group meetings to get to know your colleagues and discuss projects.

5. Digital Communication and Collaboration Tools:

• Familiarize yourself with the virtual tools used for communication, project management, and team collaboration.

• Learn how to navigate video conferencing, chat applications, and document-sharing platforms.

6. Company Culture and Values in a Remote Context:

● Understand how the company's culture and values translate into a remote work environment.

● Learn how your role contributes to the company's mission and goals, even when working from a distance.

7. Performance Expectations and Goals:

● Discuss performance expectations, key performance indicators (KPIs), and milestones with your manager through virtual meetings.

● Set goals for your role and receive guidance on how to meet them remotely.

8. Regular Virtual Check-ins:

● Schedule regular virtual check-ins with your supervisor or mentor to discuss your progress, ask questions, and seek guidance.

9. Remote Social Integration:

● Engage in virtual team-building activities, online chats, or video calls to connect with your colleagues socially.

- Participate in virtual events or informal gatherings to build relationships from a distance.

10. Policies and Procedures in a Remote Context:

- Receive information about remote work policies, ethics, and code of conduct.

- Understand remote-specific policies such as communication protocols, time tracking, and work hours.

11. Ongoing Remote Support:

- Access resources for remote work best practices, time management, and maintaining work-life balance.

- Seek support and guidance from HR, IT, or your manager for technical or work-related challenges.

12. Remote Performance Evaluation and Transition:

- Undergo remote performance evaluations to assess your progress and discuss areas of improvement.

- Based on the evaluation, transition fully into your role as a remote team member.

Overall, the onboarding process in a remote setting is designed to provide you with the necessary tools, information, and support to succeed in your role while working from a distance. Effective communication, virtual training, and engagement with your remote team will be key components of your onboarding experience.

CHAPTER 7

Balancing Work and Life.

Achieving a harmonious balance between work and personal life is a vital aspect of remote work success. This section delves into strategies and practices to ensure you maintain a healthy equilibrium, enabling you to thrive both professionally and personally.

Boundaries: Defining Work Hours and Downtime.

Creating clear boundaries between work and personal time is crucial. Establish specific work hours to maintain structure and prevent work from spilling into your personal life. Equally important is designating downtime when work-related activities cease, allowing you to recharge and engage in activities that bring you joy and relaxation.

Fostering Social Connections in a Remote Environment

Remote work can sometimes lead to feelings of isolation. This subsection emphasizes the significance of nurturing social connections even when working from a distance. Discover methods to stay connected with colleagues through virtual interactions, group chats, and online team-building activities, ensuring a sense of camaraderie and inclusion.

Avoiding Burnout and Maintaining a Healthy Work-Life Balance

When you are a remote worker preventing burnout is paramount. Explore strategies to maintain a healthy work-life balance, such as time management techniques, regular breaks, and prioritizing self-care. Learn to recognize the signs of burnout and implement measures to prevent it, ensuring you sustain productivity and well-being throughout your remote work journey.

By effectively managing boundaries, fostering social connections, and prioritizing your well-being, you'll create a remote work experience that not only enhances your professional achievements but also enriches your overall quality of life.

Strategies for Balancing Remote Work, Family Life, and Parenting Responsibilities

I deliberated extensively on this particular section, as its inclusion was a last-minute decision. However, I believe it holds value for others, as it has personally aided me. Balancing remote work with family life, particularly when caring for a toddler or baby who isn't yet attending school, can present challenges and stress. Yet, through careful planning and efficient time management, the initial difficulty will give way to adjustment and improvement in your pursuits. below are strategies to guide you in skillfully navigating your work tasks, parental responsibilities, and household duties while upholding productivity:

❖ **Create a Structured Schedule**

Establish a daily routine that includes dedicated blocks of time for work, toddler care, and errands.

Allocate specific time slots for school runs, grocery shopping, and house chores to ensure they're accounted for.

❖ **Prioritize Tasks**

Identify your most important work tasks and prioritize them during periods of focused productivity.

Tackle essential house chores during breaks or when your

toddler is occupied or napping.

❖ **Utilize Naptime and Bedtime**

Make the most of your toddler's naptime and bedtime to accomplish intensive work tasks or complete household chores.

❖ **Set Boundaries and Communicate:**

Clearly communicate your work hours to your family and set expectations for when you need focused time.

Use visual cues, like a closed door or a designated workspace, to signal when you're in work mode.

❖ **Delegate and Share Responsibilities:**

Involve your partner or other family members in parenting duties and household chores to distribute the workload. Delegate tasks based on individual strengths and availability.

❖ Meal Planning and Online Shopping:

Plan meals and create a shopping list to minimize time spent on grocery shopping.

Consider online grocery delivery services to save time and avoid trips to the store.

❖ Batch Tasks:

Group similar errands, such as school runs and grocery shopping, on specific days to consolidate outings.

Batch processing house chores to efficiently complete them in one go.

❖ Self-Care and Breaks:

Prioritize self-care by incorporating short breaks for yourself during the day to recharge.

Use breaks for relaxation, stretching, or quick household tasks.

❖ Engage Your Toddler in Chores:

Involve your toddler in simple household tasks to foster a sense of responsibility and spend quality time together.

Plan Family Time:

It is important to dedicate uninterrupted family time

during evenings and weekends to strengthen your bond with your toddler and partner.

Remember that achieving a balance between remote work, family life, and parenting is an ongoing process. Be flexible, adapt to changes, and celebrate small victories as you manage your roles effectively and create a nurturing environment for both your career and your family.

CONCLUSION

In conclusion, navigating the realm of remote work requires a comprehensive understanding of various elements that contribute to a successful and fulfilling virtual career. Throughout this guide, we have explored a wide range of topics aimed at empowering you to excel in a remote work environment. Let's revisit the key takeaways that have been highlighted:

Remote Work Advantages: We've uncovered the benefits of remote work, including flexibility, work-life balance, and the potential to thrive in a location-independent setting.

Effective Time Management: Mastering time management techniques ensure optimal productivity, allowing you to strike a balance between work tasks and personal activities.

Optimized Virtual Workspace: Crafting an organized and ergonomically sound workspace enhances focus, creativity, and overall work efficiency.

Networking and Building a Remote Career: Embracing online

platforms, cultivating a personal brand, and navigating remote interviews are essential for forging a successful remote career path

Importance of Ergonomics and Well-being: Prioritizing physical health, movement, mental well-being, and stress relief fosters a holistic approach to remote work.

Balancing Work and Life: Setting boundaries, fostering social connections, and avoiding burnout contribute to a harmonious work-life balance.

Continuous Learning and Adaptation: Embrace ongoing learning, stay updated on industry trends, and remain adaptable to the evolving landscape of remote work.

Finally, it's important to emphasize the idea of "Embracing the Future of Work." This concept encourages us to welcome the changes and opportunities that working from a distance brings. Much like we adapt to new experiences, embracing the future of remote work means being open to using technology to connect with colleagues, finding ways to stay productive, and being positive about the evolving landscape of work. By embracing this future, we position ourselves to thrive in a world where remote work is an integral part of how we achieve our goals and contribute to our careers.

ABOUT THE AUTHOR

Amber Willie

But Amber Willie does not simply stop at the pursuit of knowledge for its own sake. Her enduring commitment to sharing her findings, insights, and wisdom through her writing underscores her fundamental belief in the transformative power of information. With every word she pens, she seeks to empower readers like you to advance in your chosen field, enrich your understanding, and, most importantly, provide tangible value to others through the application of newfound knowledge.

www.ingramcontent.com/pod-product-compliance
Lightning Source LLC
Chambersburg PA
CBHW062255290526
45794CB00006B/2560